She's Not Heavy. She's my Sis.

Marci Blum, OSF

BH
PUBLISHING

She's Not Heavy. She's my Sis.

Author Marci Blum OSF
Copyright © 2012 BHC Publishing

Selected poems from:

Mary Oliver. New and Selected Poems. Boston: Beacon Press, 1992.

Diedrich Bonhoeffer. Letters and Papers from Prison (1943-45). MacMillan Publishing Company, Inc., 1961.

Edward Hays. Prayers For the Domestic Church. Easten, Kansas: Shantivanam House of Prayer, 1979.

BHC Publishing, LLC, Bellevue, Iowa

BHC
PUBLISHING

Printed in the United States of America
First Printing: November 2012
ISBN 978-0-9827772-5-1

Acknowledgements

Thank you for reading this book about a spiritual journey with a dog. People have asked me when the book would be published as some expressed a loss of their beloved pet. Candice Chaloupka read the manuscript and graciously offered to publish the book.

I especially want to thank my parents, Ina (Bauerly) and Edwin Blum, who first allowed me to have a dog when I was a child. I am grateful to my sister and brother-in-law. Lucille and George Heenan took care of Sis and Rhea many times. Their dogs, Mitzi, Ginger and Johnny mentored Sis by teaching her proper manners in behavior. My older sister and her husband, Vanita and Jack Raymond graciously welcomed Sis and Rhea into their home on visits.

I am grateful to my Franciscan Sisters who lived with Sis—Irene Hellman, Janice Rosman, Margaret Burkle, Susan Ivis and Angie Freking—at different times of her life. They lived with her antics and stayed with her when I was gone. I am indebted to Marie Cigrand OSF with whom I live. Marie took care of Rhea when I was not at home and graciously did the proofreading of this book, along with Elvira Kelley, OSF.

I am grateful to the wonderful care of the veterinarians throughout Sis' life and a special veterinarian and friend in Waterloo, Dr. Brad Kneeland, who diagnosed Rhea's heart condition and graciously provided her with heart medications. I cannot forget the loving care and patience of Teri Olson, Sis' and Rhea's dog groomer at Groomingdales in Dubuque.

It is a gift to receive God's care from a four-legged. And Sis, thanks for being there for me.

Author's Note

While carrying my 25-pound dog in her later years of her life, someone approached me asking, "Isn't she heavy?" I recalled the words of Father Ed Flanagan, founder of Boys Town in Omaha, who said, "He's not heavy; he's my brother." I looked at my pet and thought to myself, "She's not heavy. She's my Sister." I welcomed a four-legged animal into my life and she changed my life considerably.

Sr. Marci with Sis (3 years old).

She Probably Needs a Dog

In one of Charles Schultz's Peanuts cartoons, a friend of Charlie Brown asks where Marci is. He points to Marci who is sleeping on the sofa. Marci has been under a lot of stress and Charlie Brown feels his friend is too hard on herself. Snoopy peers around the sofa and says, "She probably needs a dog."

So begins my story. While coordinating faith formation in a Minneapolis suburban parish, I was living alone in a convent on the premises of the church grounds. The former farmhouse encompassed five bedrooms, two baths, a library, living and dining rooms, kitchen and a chapel.

Although I had family and friends nearby for socializing, loneliness sometimes gripped me in the evenings after work. I tried to occupy my time with reading, watching television, visiting friends or talking on the phone. Eventually I would be alone again with nothing to do but stare at the walls or read the same paragraph in a book.

I had to make a decision for a direction in my life. Should I remain in the ministry I was in or return to living in community with the other Sisters? I was pulled in both directions. I enjoyed my work with the people and liked to organize and plan programs. Yet I missed the companionship in the house as I had experienced in my former places of ministry.

One Sunday, after reading the headline news and comics, I randomly scanned the want-ads. I spied an advertisement that a family had six pups available. Out of curiosity, I drove to the house to "just look" at the puppies. The pups were a mixed breed of a llasa apsa and a poodle. Llasa-poo was what the owner called them.

The six pups immediately crawled over me as I sat on the floor playing with them. Their short attention span led them to another place to play but one came back, crawled into my lap and fell asleep. "It looks like she chose you," the owner said.

The sleeping puppy was mostly black with a white star on her head, a white patch on her chest and white on her four toes. "Quite cute," I murmured to myself.

I pondered what the owner said, "It looks like she chose you." Was I really going to do this? I was overwhelmed. How will I be able to take care of her when I am gone on business and family trips? How will I be able to financially pay the veterinarian bills? What if I neglect to pay sufficient attention to her? What if I live communally with other Sisters and they do not accept her?

I had to be practical but personal needs had led me to the pup's home. I needed companionship. I needed someone to greet me at the door. I needed a companion to walk. Peace with the decision finally came. I accepted that I needed a companion to be present with me, to meet my needs of loneliness. I wanted a pet to take care of.

I was willing to take the risk of adopting the pup. It is a risk to say "yes," to trust that all will be well. The pup chose me and my life has never been the same. I chose to be claimed.

The day was Groundhog Day, February 2, 1984. I did not see a shadow of a groundhog that day. Instead, I saw the shadow of a pup lying on my lap in the car on the one-hour drive home. When I arrived, she was so scared to leave my lap. It was so new for a six-week puppy seeing a new environment, no other four-leggeds around, no mother dog, no familiar surroundings.

I had no preparations ready to bring a puppy into the house. I quickly set up a box with a blanket on the kitchen floor, spread newspapers to catch those spills, filled a dish with water and barricaded the kitchen doorway with a chair. I made a quick run to the store for dog food.

My first night with a new puppy was short on sleep. She whined and cried all night long in the kitchen. I tucked a ticking clock in her bed so she could imagine being comforted by her mother's heart beat.

The second night she laid on a blanket on top of my bed until she fell asleep; then I gently carried her to her bed in the kitchen. In the early morning hours I was awakened to whines again. After several nights of this, I relented and let her sleep on my bed, where she continued to sleep for seventeen years. Needless to say, I have had some sleepless nights in a twin bed with a dog at my side or feet.

A six week puppy is quite young to bring home. Usually not weaned from the mother, the puppy would nuzzle one of my fingers, seeking the comfort of her mother's milk, while sitting in my lap. Through the weeks she gradually let go of this need for her mother's milk.

Naming my new companion was another issue. In the book, *The Little Prince* by Saint-Exupery, the fox said to the little boy, "You are responsible for what you have tamed." I thought to myself, "We are also responsible for what we have named." As I looked at the black six-week-old pup with a white star on her forehead and chest, and with white spots on her feet, she appeared to be similar in color as her birth mother. I observed her antics and movements. No name came to mind.

From when I was a child, I had a fascination with St. Francis of Assisi, a saint imbued with the love of creation. Francis wrote that we are all creatures of God. Since God created us as God's own, we are all brothers and sisters with God as our Creator. Francis called the wolf, Brother Wolf, the rabbit, Brother Rabbit, the sun, Brother Sun, the moon, Sister Moon. We are in relationship with all that lives. Impelled by Francis' vision, I named her "Sister Dog," "Sis" for short. When one is named, one is tamed.

A Rambunctious Dog

Snoopy's assessment of his experience with Charlie Brown in Charles Schultz' cartoon says it all. Snoopy muses, "I wonder why some of us were born dogs while others were born people. Is it just pure chance or what is it? Sometimes the whole thing doesn't seem very fair. Why should I have been the lucky one?"

I often wondered the same question—who was the lucky one—Sis or me? Sis was full of life, like the world revolved around her, somewhat like a toddler. For myself, I knew inside that Sis gave me life.

Sis was an impetuous pup, full of energy and with a mind of her own. I could not trust her to be outdoors without a leash. She liked to run, curious to find anything that she could put into her mouth. To offset her energy, we walked daily; on some days, several walks. On our walks, people marveled at her cute features. They even inquired if I would consider breeding her.

During the day when I was at work, Sis was confined to the kitchen. One day when I returned home from work, I found no Sis in the kitchen. In a panic, I searched the house, following the evidence of enjoyed freedom to her hiding under the dining room table.

In the chapel, potted plants were toppled on the carpet; at least five potted plants upended in one room. Sis ran out of the room and hid as I shrieked. It was a long time before she touched a plant.

Her next adventure with plants occurred when she discovered the huge potted cactus plant in the upstairs room. Her curious nature led her astray again. The painful (and surprised) yelp led me to Sis. She did not run this time. The evidence was on her nose. Sis was not a happy camper, nor was I. She did not want to sit still as I worked on removing the cactus stickers from her nose. This time, she seemed to have learned a lesson—never again did she touch the cactus plant.

By this time, Sis was four months old. People continued to ask me to breed her so they could have one of her pups. Not wanting to deal with the birthing process, I decided to have her fixed. Shortly after the appointment was made, I returned home from work to find blood on the kitchen floor. It was her time.

I phoned the veterinarian with the news. Sis could still have the surgery but it would cost more. I decided to wait three weeks. When I say three weeks, I mean three *long* weeks! Five hundred and four hours of being on guard.

Male dogs appeared at the door day and night yelping for Sis. Sis barked at the door and windows wanting to go outside. Some of the hopeful suitors must have come from other neighborhoods as I had never seen some dogs who came to "visit" Sis. Dog breeders tell me that male dogs pick up the scent of a female dog from quite a distance. Was it ever true! Sis did not go outside without her leash and me. When we did walk, we walked quickly. During these *long* weeks, Sis was careful in keeping herself clean but I still needed to wash her blanket periodically.

After Sis' spay operation, she slept just as anyone after a traumatic surgery. For several days she was touchy and

cranky. She wanted to be alone. Her pain was more than
enough to handle, so I let her be.

When Sis recovered from her surgery, she became her
old self again. She was rambunctious and free-spirited. It
was not surprising to find my slippers or shoes with teeth
marks on them. One slipper was unredeemable.

Sis also seemed to have selective hearing. She came to
me when it was *her* time, not my time. Her refusal to come
when called happened one time too many. Frustrated, I
would go into the house, thinking she would follow. She
did not follow. I tried bribery, tempting her with a small
scoop of ice cream. That was the ticket! Sis came to eat the
ice cream and I would grab her collar! Success was short
lived; Sis caught on.

It soon became a game. She would refuse to come, I
would put out the bowl of ice cream, but one time when
I reached for her collar, Sis dodged my hand. She looked
at me as if saying, "Gotcha." Sheepishly, I realized that she
had gotten the best of me. Bribery would not work but
something had to be done. I knew that someone had to
learn some skills at obedience. That was me. Those who
have pups know that dog obedience is for the owners, not
solely for the canines.

When Sis turned five months, I made the decision that
would be a turning point in her life and mine. We would
attend ten weeks of dog obedience school, together, of course.

Sis and I went to dog obedience school to learn the skills
of coming when called, heeling when walking, walking with
a leash without Sis biting it or pulling me along, greeting
other dogs in a hospitable manner, sitting with a command,
standing with a command, lying down with a command. An
ideal that was not achieved totally in ten weeks.

In the first class, we were taught that dogs need to
socialize with other dogs. In a circle facing each other,
dogs on leash, we would let the dogs greet each other. That

looked easy enough. All was going well until the end when Sis greeted a dog and pooped.

Totally embarrassed, I let the dog trainer know. "No problem," she said, "dogs will do that when they get excited or stressed."

We were told to practice every day what we learned. The mantra from dog obedience school echoed within me as I worked with Sis: "The hand that pets is not the hand that hits."

I dutifully practiced with Sis for her to come when called. It was a great feat when she did come—with an offer of a treat. After many months, success came when Sis heeled beside me when walking. Sometimes I would take the leash off her and she stayed with me walking beside me. "Good girl, Sis" became my chant when success occurred.

I continued my daily exercise walks with Sis. People continued to offer comments. "Isn't she cute." "What a nice looking dog."

Hunter Instincts—But "Not Yet"

One evening when Sis went outside, I discovered another side of her. After relieving herself, she barked at the door to come in. I, dutifully trained, opened the door and saw she was carrying something in her mouth. I told her to drop it. She did. A dead rat was lying on the living room carpet.

Needless to say, the rat was shoveled into the garbage can. Why did Sis bring in a dead rat? I hope she was not capable of killing it, as our neighbors had outdoor cats. Through inquiry from other dog owners, I learned that dogs will carry back to the owners a dead animal to appease the "alpha dog" owner.

A dog by nature and breed is a hunter. Sis tried hard to live up to her pedigree and species. As a pup, under the age of two, she believed that squirrels were made to be chased.

One day when we were in the yard, she saw a squirrel running around. She immediately gave chase. The squirrel scurried up a tree. What did my eyes behold but Sis barking up the wrong tree! Wherever we walked, Sis made sure the squirrels and birds in her sight were off the ground.

On the other hand, Sis was a cautious hunter. Sis and I were home alone one evening. Out of the corner of my eye I saw Sis amble over to the basement door and sniff underneath the door. She barked, which aroused my curiosity to open the basement door. I heard a noise and quickly closed the door. Should I call 911? I told myself to be brave. Sis was right beside me pushing against my leg.

Cautiously I re-opened the door and moved slowly down the basement steps. There it was. A bat was flying back and forth, back and forth. I screeched and ran up the stairs and into the living room with Sis at my heels. The bat flew up the steps from the basement and followed us. I then ran into the kitchen with Sis and the bat behind us. The great escape took place. I ran outdoors with Sis following. It seemed incongruous that we were outdoors and the bat indoors!

I ran nonstop to my neighbor's house down the block. As a former Marine, he steadfastly trounced into the house and looked for the bat. It was nowhere to be found. After extensive searching, the bat was found in a plant hanging in my bedroom. I did not want the bat killed, so the man kindly released it outdoors where it belonged. Sis and I stayed indoors with the bat outside where it belonged.

When Sis was six years old, she carried on her hunting expeditions. In the early evening before dark, she came inside with a little dead rabbit. I did not reward her nor did I scold her. It was her nature to hunt. Yet, being an animal rights advocate, I could not praise her. So I scooped up the rabbit for burial.

Animal behaviorists write that dogs are like wolves and hunt in packs. Dogs in a pack will bring back a dead prey for reward to the leader dog or alpha dog. She was doing what God created her to do—to survive and socially bond.

In walking one afternoon with Sis, she was off in a flash. I sped after her and found her in a yard scurrying after a ground squirrel. Watching her, she caught the ground squirrel and played with it by throwing it in the air and letting it fall. I stopped the hunting game, retrieved Sis and left the ground squirrel looking at me out of the corner of its eye.

Sis was sometimes successful with squirrels, but cats were a different story. Once a cat ambled across our yard. I watched Sis to see what she would do. With her nose to the ground she stealthily crept towards the cat. Sis was not as stealthy as she thought. The cat, with hair raised, spit and hissed as she continued to walk. Sis kept her distance.

Sometimes Sis would forget her training. Her mind would be so set on chasing squirrels, that her selective hearing would kick in and she would fail to return when called. Giving up, I would go inside and watch for her. She would return minutes later, barking to come inside. She knew where to go when she had finished her hunting spree.

Thank God she was on a leash the time a friend was taking her outdoors for an evening stroll. Hearing my friend shriek, I ran outside wondering what was going on. Sis was chasing a skunk beside the house. Luckily, my friend clasped the leash tightly as Sis strained to get her prey. To no avail. Whew.

In all her hunting escapades, Sis tried to be true to her nature—she was a hunter. Although she was not always successful (thank God), she was faithful to who she was—a dog.

A Faithful Companion

"Nothing is more comforting than sitting with your faithful dog in your lap." So says Charlie Brown about his dog, Snoopy. His dog, Snoopy has a different thought, "This is murder. My back is killing me and all four legs are asleep."

To be faithful is to be a companion. To be a companion is to be faithful. Dogs by nature are social. They have evolved from wolf packs. Wolves band together, bringing prey to be shared with the wolf pack as well as looking out for the young wolves. The elders teach the young ones to hunt and to be cautious. Dogs have acquired the social companionship from their ancestors.

An example of dogs faithful to each other is the story of Mitzi and Sis. My sister's dog, Mitzi, older than Sis, taught Sis to behave when she was a puppy. Although Mitzi was smaller in size, Sis obeyed her because dogs sense the rank of seniority. Sis was so rambunctious in playing with Mitzi that she would turn around and lean her rear in Mitzi's face. My sister called her "Sister Fanny." Mitzi would calm Sis down by growling and placing her head on top of Sis' back. Sis would then cower and be still. Both Sis and Mitzi were the best of friends. Sis would run into their house, look in the corners for dog treats that Mitzi hid and carry them in her mouth to be devoured immediately. Sis and Mitzi often walked together on the trails, truly companions on the journey.

Sis and I grew in faithful companionship. She accompanied me on my business and family car trips. I learned not to pack the night before I left, for Sis would eye the travel bags very cautiously. She would either lie beside them or pace restlessly in the house or she would dash outdoors undetected and hide behind the rear tires. When I opened the car door, all I would see was a blur as Sis jumped into the back seat.

On my visits home to see my parents, Sis accompanied me on the front seat of the car. I remember the first time I brought her home as a very young puppy. Dad asked me, "Where is she going to sleep?" I responded, "On my bed." Dad scoffed. My parents had grown up on the farm and dogs stayed outside. The family had moved to town before I was born. I was allowed to have dogs when I was a youngster. The dogs could play in the house but they slept in the garage during the warmer months and on the porch during the colder months of the year.

Later that day my dad took his usual afternoon nap. Sure enough. Sis jumped on top of his bed and slept beside him curled up by his legs. Dad felt a warm body beside him, woke up, looked at Sis, grunted and fell back asleep. It became a regular pattern for Dad to share his bed with Sis for his afternoon siestas.

Whenever I stayed overnight in a motel on my business travels, Sis would accompany me when a dog sitter was not available. I spoke to Sis beforehand about good behavior—no barking or messing. It was amazing how she maintained her equilibrium. She was a model of good behavior with no motel complaints or pet deposits.

Others sometimes joined us on our trips. Whether they were dog lovers or not, they soon became Sis lovers. Sis would sit right beside them on the car seat and cuddle up to them, placing her head on their lap. One little girl reminds me of the time when she and Sis were sitting in the back seat of the car. The girl leaned forward to talk to her mother who was in the front seat and when the girl leaned back to her seat, Sis was lying on her spot.

I often took Sis with me to the grocery store. She waited patiently in the car until I returned. One day her patience turned into visible enthusiasm in seeing me emerge from the store. I heard the car horn. Several of us looked to my car. There Sis was behind the driver's wheel. She was on her hind legs with her front paws on the steering wheel. As she leaned over the wheel, she touched the horn. It created a laughable scene for us to see a dog "driving the car."

At times I was unable to take Sis with me when I went to meetings. It was uncanny how she sensed when I was leaving. At the time when I needed to leave, Sis would run to the door to bark or to go outside. Thinking that it was great that she would be conscientious to relieve herself before I left, I let her outside. When it came time for me to go, I called for her and she would not come back inside the house. Try as I might, she would not come near me. I either had to trick her with a treat to get the leash on her or run the "racetrack" to get her.

In the house Sis was like a shadow. She would follow me in the bathroom and wait patiently. She did not like the basement so she sat at the top of the stairs until I came up. At night when she felt it was time to go to bed, she sat before me, looked intently, nudged me with her nose and barked once sharply. I would then get up and go to the bedroom and she jumped onto the bed ready for sleep.

Charles Schultz' cartoon of Charlie Brown and Snoopy resonates with me. In this particular cartoon, Charlie Brown is lying in bed with Snoopy lying on top of him. Charlie Brown says that he is lying in bed awake at night in the dark and a voice comes to him saying, "You have a dog…be happy."

Those who have experience with dogs know they are dependent on their human companions, not only for food and water and shelter, but also for affection and attention.

To determine if a dog trusts you, a dog will lie on their back with their tummy open to you. Sis was no exception. She would also jump onto the sofa next to you to cuddle. At night, she would cuddle up like a warm comforter, pushing against my back for warmth. She was like a furnace, warming me too. My heating bill went down during the winter months!

A dog can teach us to trust in a higher power. The word, DOG is an acronym for "Depend on God." We can look at a dog and remember God—to trust and depend on God. Remember, DOG spelled backwards is GOD! A dog reminds us that God is ever faithful on our spiritual journey.

It is wholesome to have a companion through life. Dogs remind us that we are social, that we are relational. Wherever I went, Sis was sure to go, or wanted to. Loneliness disappears when a dog is around. I felt secure when she was there. When I could not find her outside, I panicked and yelled louder for her. She would come running when she heard the panic in my voice. We needed each other. That is what companions do for each other.

Fun and Games

Dogs like to play "hide and seek" as well as "catch me if you can." Sis was a pro at these games. Outdoors we played tag. I would chase her and she skirted corners and hid under and behind bushes and trees. Then we would reverse the play. She would chase me. I actually hid behind buildings or doors and would jump out and scare her. She would run and the game was reversed.

Sis was a teaser as well. I learned to anticipate her teasing. Her favorite game was to sit and watch me change from my work clothes to leisure attire. As soon as I laid my clothing on the bed, she would jump up, grab it, and run out of the room. She would hide under the table watching me and waiting for me to retrieve the article of clothing from her. Sis would play this game with others who lived in the house. One of my housemates literally ran up the stairs yelling after Sis, "Give me back my clothes."

Even in winter Sis was active in playing this "game." She would meet me at the door and immediately grab my gloves and scurry away. I would chase her throughout the house while she hid under the table and chairs in one room after another. Although she was panting, she would never surrender the gloves unless I forcefully took them from her. Sometimes she would drop the gloves if she saw I was distracted with something else. Many a tattered glove found its way into the wastebasket.

Besides her games with me, Sis enjoyed her toys, especially stuffed animals. She did not like the rubber or squeaky toys; she loved the teddy bears and the plush animals. One particular stuffed animal, a dog, became her sleeping companion. She would carry it to her blanket and fall asleep with the stuffed animal in her mouth.

Sis loved to chew, like a baby cutting teeth. Beef jerky was a delicacy for her. She would transfer her chewable treats to chewable objects. Sis would gnaw and gnaw at her stuffed animals until the inner stuffing came out. It was a real discovery when more and more cotton inside was emptied. I would put the stuffing back inside the toy and sew it up. Sure enough, she would undo the sewing and out came the stuffing—again and again.

Sis really loved stuffed animals, not just her own! One day while walking, we came upon a mother and her four-year-old boy carrying his teddy bear. Sis went right up to the boy and grabbed his teddy bear. The boy held on tightly. They tugged away until I intervened and pulled Sis away. How does one explain to a little boy that a dog wants to play with his teddy bear?

Three little girls came to the door one afternoon inquiring, "Can Sis come out to play?" With a smile on my face, I turned around to Sis behind me and asked her, "Sis, do you want to go out to play?" I opened the door and Sis went outdoors with the little girls. Sometime later, I heard the doorbell. The little girls at the door said, "Sis wants to come in now." So I opened the door and Sis came in. What do children and dogs have in common? Play.

With a playfulness comes dancing. Sometimes I would dance to music I played while at home. Sis would jump on me and surround my legs, wanting to join in on the fun. I would hold her front legs so she could dance on her back legs with me. It did not matter if it was slow or fast music. She would dance to the movement. Often we would dance to the music, but sometimes we would sing.

I play the guitar for recreation. Whenever I strummed the guitar and sang, Sis would prick up her ears, look at me, then break into "song." She opened her mouth, elevated her head and out came a howl! When I quit strumming, she stopped "singing."

Playing was so much a part of Sis. I learned a lot about the need to play from her. People ignore this imporant need. We tell ourselves "we don't have time to play." We think we are too busy to relax and have fun. Abraham Lincoln once said that we are not to take life too seriously as we will not get out of life alive anyway. (I wonder if he learned that from a dog?) Dogs can teach us to take time to enjoy the moment—now.

To play is to be ourselves. Hang around with a dog and learn to be natural.

Gestures of Hospitality

If you ever have times where you need to feel welcomed and wanted, you need a dog. A dog is a "welcome mat" at the door. I could be gone for one hour or eight hours; it didn't matter. Sis was at the door waiting.

Sis stood so close to the door, she would have to move so I could enter. She wiggled back and forth, tail wagging in excitement and she would grin. Yes, her mouth would go up and a smile appeared. I looked forward to going home, knowing she was waiting for me.

Sis did display her displeasure with me for not being home when she felt I needed to be. When I was gone for a week, I returned to a seemingly empty house. The dog-sitter was there but I could not find Sis. I looked everywhere. I finally found her underneath my bed. She refused to come out for five hours. I pleaded with treats but to no avail. It was her way to disapprove of my absence.

Sis would welcome other people into the house. She sensed if someone was approaching the house and barked to announce their presence before I heard them.

Sis remembered friends who had not been by in a while. She would still greet them with wiggles and wagging; dogs do have memories.

When dogs are not welcoming to others, it is not that they are mean-spirited by nature. I believe God made all creatures as loving. An all-good God can only create creatures reflective of the Creator. Animals, like humans, hunt when they need to survive or protect themselves if threatened. If dogs are hostile, it is due to poor training or abuse. Is that similar to us in our upbringing and behavior?

We may not be able to wiggle our bodies to greet but we shake hands. We may not be able to speak in the same language but we can smile. We may not be able to wag our tails but we can hug each other. Dogs teach us to welcome.

A Charles Schultz cartoon features Linus sharing with Charlie Brown and Lucy that he had to admit to the teacher that he just didn't know the answer. Charlie Brown responds by saying that some questions don't have an answer. Lucy questions, "Like what?" Snoopy has the answer with a question, "Like did Jesus ever own a dog?"

I like to imagine Jesus welcomed dogs.

A Caring Presence

When I am depressed or have experienced a setback in my life, I have appreciated a caring presence. Sis was there. Sis seemed to know those times when I needed TLC (tender loving care). She would sidle up to me, rubbing her body against me to get my attention. She would jump on my lap. She would lick my face. She would stay close to me for a length of time needed to allay frustration or heartache.

When a roommate came home from work one evening, she was low in spirits. Her workday did not go well and she sat on the sofa sharing what happened with tears in her eyes. Out of nowhere Sis jumped on her lap. She absently petted Sis while she was talking. Later in the evening she told me Sis had been a big help. She said, "When I was petting Sis, it seemed like my anxiety diminished and a peacefulness came over me."

On another evening five of us were praying. Sis was known for interrupting prayer with her shrill bark. I figured she felt we were not paying enough attention to her. Our prayer that night was a birthday celebration with a guest in attendance. Sis lay on the floor as we prayed. I kept glancing over at Sis, who was actually quiet. She was lying on her front paws, her front right paw was laid over her front left paw, like she was praying with us. After prayer, our guest was so impressed with Sis' praying behavior. If only she knew other times.

When we need companions to care for us, it seems someone comes into our lives unexpectedly. A dog reminds us to open our eyes and our hearts to receive.

What Can We Learn from Dogs

A dog calls us to be true to ourselves. A dog is a dog is a dog. A dog is a creature of habit. Whenever Sis would lie down she would first circle round and round to make her bed. She would hide treats under chairs or would dig in the carpet, lay her treat down, then push invisible dirt over the treat with her nose to hide it. Sis would carry her dog dish over to where I was sitting and then begin to eat.

A dog likes routine. It seems like a dog knows when it is time for meals. Sis would approach me either with her tongue wiping her mouth or she would nose me to get my attention.

Occasionally I would stay up past ten o'clock bedtime. Sis would again get my attention by pushing her nose against my leg or a short yip to move me in the direction of the bedroom. She would then jump on the bed and wait for me to shut off the light.

That is what a dog does. That is what a dog is. Dogs can teach us to be who we are, not who we are not.

Fear and Courage

Dogs can be courageous but still feel fear, like humans. On one of my visits home during the summer, my mom, dad and I were sitting on lawn chairs in their backyard while Sis nosed around the yard. We heard barking but it was not coming from Sis.

Two big dogs from an adjoining yard were bounding towards Sis. She looked up and ran towards me, landing on my lap, as if I were her savior. She peered plaintively at me as if to say, "Help me." The two big dogs retreated.

One afternoon Sis and I were walking. A German Shepherd appeared out of nowhere and rushed at us barking. Fearing for Sis, I immediately picked her up. While holding her, I said to the bigger dog, "No. Go home." With that, I turned around and walked quickly away with the bigger dog looking at us.

It was common for Sis to bark at other dogs when they came near. Whether Sis barked out of fear or courage, I do not know, but sometimes she growled out of jealousy to keep another dog from coming too near to me. Dogs do protect their turf whether it is their yard or owner.

It was uncanny to observe Sis when she did bark at other dogs. She barked and barked and then she turned to see if I was around. If she saw me move in her direction, she would be more courageous and move forward to continue barking. If I did not move, she remained still.

Sis was brave in the car, so brave that she would bark at horses and cows through the open window as long as they were at a distance. However, when we walked on the country roads and Sis met the same four-leggeds, she would cower and stay close to me, not barking.

When Sis was older, she was attacked by a German Shepherd while she was in the yard. I had let her outside one morning but quickly ran out when I heard a yip. I found the large dog standing over her. Sis was on her back, legs in the air, maintaining a submissive position. I yelled at the dog who thankfully ran off.

~

Perhaps it was due to the stress in her older age, but Sis developed yeast infection, requiring a trip to the pharmacy.

Sis was usually afraid to go to the veterinarian and even to the dog groomer. As we neared the door, Sis would tremble as I held her in my arms. If she were on a leash, she would pull back and freeze trying to stop forward movement. The vet and groomer would try to coax her into their chambers with a treat, but Sis was having none of it!

I would reassure her, "It's okay, Sis" in a gentle soothing voice. When it was all over, with bows on her ears from the groomer, she bounded out of the chambers ready to be safe at home.

People say that fear is courage deep within. Heroes tell us that their actions originate from fear of danger. It is paradoxical that courage comes from fear. Fear is an instinctual sense of survival. Fear is a helpful tool to protect us from what can be harmful. Fear helps us to decide to stay or flee. A companion also helps us when we need someone. A companion is someone we can run to for support and care.

Finding Strength in Hostile Actions

Sometimes we get hurt or we are a victim of hostility. Sis was no exception, despite her being a dog. Election Day, November 1985, was a windy and bleak autumn day. I was raking the back yard while Sis played outside with me.

Since she was so good about staying within my sight, I did not have her on a leash. I noticed she was walking from the boundary of the yard but I was distracted with filling the plastic bag with leaves before they blew away.

I heard a loud bang, thinking that it probably was the backfire of a car. I continued to rake. Moments later Sis was at my side trembling. I picked her up and felt something wet and warm. I looked down and saw there was blood all over Sis and now, all over me. Adrenalin pumping, I walked over to a wooden fence behind our house to peek through a hole in the fence. I could see two men working on a car in their driveway. I could see no one else in the area.

Resolutely, I crawled through the fence hole and asked the men if they had heard a gunshot. They both shook their heads "no" but did not look at me. "My dog was shot a few minutes ago," I continued. "Are you sure you didn't hear a gun shot?" They did not respond as they continued to work on the car, ignoring me.

Refusing to be intimidated, I told them that if anything happened to my dog, I would be talking to them. I telephoned the veterinarian who told me to bring her in immediately. I dropped her off but within an hour the vet called for permission to operate. Sis had a fever of 105 degrees, three degrees above normal for a dog.

The vet encouraged me to report the incident to the police. Feeling it was partly my fault for allowing Sis to wander into the neighbor's yard, I hesitated. When the vet told me it was illegal to fire a weapon within city limits, I made the call.

The police sent an officer to investigate. The officer spoke with the two men but they denied shooting Sis. They did have numerous guns. I found out later these same men sold guns and the police department was a customer.

The officer also pointed out there was no blood in their yard. "Of course, there was no blood, it was all over me and my dog!" I replied. "Sis was frightened, she did not hang out in their yard to bleed; she came right to me." I realized then that the mind of the officer was already decided in favor of the two men.

The vet called several hours later to report on Sis' condition. "Someone was watching over Sis," the vet informed me as he described how the bullet lodged in her intestines but stayed intact, not exploding as it was designed.

Sis returned home several days later and I nursed her for weeks giving her antibiotics and cleansing the open wound with hydrogen peroxide. The scar remained for the rest of her life, a reminder of the hostility of some people.

I was frustrated with the realization that people can get away with a crime. Wanting justice, I refused to let the issue go. I contacted the Humane Society and Grievance Court. I was told that with no witnesses nothing could be done. Still not wanting to give up, I hoped a personal visit with the chief of police might help.

The police chief was not in the office so I met with the sergeant. I described the incident to the sergeant who then took his gun from his holster. He said, "I know that guy. He sold me this gun." I responded, "It must be hard to work on a case when the suspect is a friend of yours." Visibly angry, he retorted, "Are you saying I'm not doing my job?" He threw my bullet, my only evidence, across the room. I picked it up and left.

Having no recourse for justice, I was left to wonder how I would pay the $200 vet bill? Thankfully, a postcard advertising a job delivering city telephone books arrived in the mail. For a month I delivered phone books with the help of my friends. I was able to earn enough money to pay the vet for Sis and the chiropractor needed for me after a month of carrying the heavy load!

I wish I could say the shooting was the only pain Sis had to suffer, but the next year she was a victim of hostility again. Sis and I were walking through a city park when a big dog approached and lunged at Sis. I immediately stood between Sis and her attacker, kicking at the dog to ward off the attack. Sis lay still on the ground like an opossum.

A young woman came rushing up with a muzzle and tried to hold the dog so I could pick Sis up. The dog, however, lunged towards Sis, biting her in her stomach. I found myself covered in Sis' blood, again. Finally, the young woman succeeded in muzzling the dog. I demanded to know why the dog was running unleashed, unmuzzled through a public park.

I wish I could say her reply provided some comfort. She said, "I didn't see you in the park. My dog is supposed to have his muzzle on at all times since he has a tendency to attack small dogs. He had a small dog at the throat one time. I adopted him at a humane society not too long ago. He's part wolf." She said this so casually, as if she did not realize the seriousness of her dog's actions. She did offer to go with us to the vet and she did pay the bill. Again, I applied hydrogen peroxide to Sis' wound and administered antibiotics.

Sis healed again but the next incident was not from a hostile neighbor or vicious dog. She was injured by someone I should have been able to trust. Sis is part poodle and required a higher level of maintenance with her grooming than I could provide. So Sis would go to the groomer every so often. She would get washed and combed, her ears were cleaned, nails cut, and hair trimmed around her eyes. After one appointment, I picked her up and noticed one eye was shut.

Again, we went to the veterinarian who informed me that the outer layer of Sis' retina was damaged. Once again, I played nurse and applied medication—eye drops twice daily for weeks.

These incidents were storms not only in Sis' life but also in mine. It was only by a power greater than me that I was able to weather these storms. These incidents taught me how little control we really have in our lives. But in our vulnerability we are strengthened. By the grace of God, we are given the courage to endure and to cope.

Life is a trust walk. A life journey consists of detours, pits and deserts, yet with a landscape of valleys and oases. Beyond the clouds a sun is shining. Sis endured her suffering. I was beside her tending to her medical needs. That is what we are there for in life—to be companions with and for each other.

A Healthy Way of Life from Living with a Dog

If one wants to stay healthy, get a pet. Dogs, in particular, motivate us to choose a healthy lifestyle. Medical experts tell us we need discipline to keep a balanced routine in our lives. "Early to bed and early to rise make a person healthy, wealthy and wise." A dog helps us live that proverb.

When Sis needed to relieve herself in the early morning she would get restless in my bed. If I did not heed her movements she would bark. If that did not get me up, she would stand over me, her face in mine. Her last resort was to lick my face. Thanks to Sis, I did not need an alarm clock. To this day, I wake up faithfully at six a.m.

Getting out of the house is also important for a healthy outlook. Having cabin fever, in the midst of winter, is impossible when one has a dog. A dog needs to be taken outside umpteen times a day.

Waiting for Sis to relieve herself was tedious. She had to find that one particular blade of grass. This offered me the opportunity to really observe the outside world. I began to notice things around me that I never knew existed.

One morning while waiting for Sis, I noticed two earthworms in the yard. One worm emerged from the ground twelve inches from the other worm. They crawled towards each other and embraced for the longest time. Another time I was able to watch a hummingbird feed and flap her wings numerous times in midair.

An inner sense of well-being and peacefulness engulfs me when I am in nature. I discovered, thanks to Sis, that being still and watching nature is like a meditation for the soul. A dog can lead us to wonder.

Exercise is also an essential part of a healthy lifestyle and dogs love to exercise. Going for a walk is among the top three favorite activities for a dog. Sis was no exception.

When Sis wanted to go for a walk, she would sit in front of me and stare. If that did not get my attention, she would bark. Not just any bark, a high staccato bark that would make me jump up!

I had to be careful of certain words, like "walk," or "ride." Dogs are smart. They pick up on words that concern them. When Sis heard one of those words, she would go crazy; jumping, running to the door, even pulling on my pant leg to get me moving.

Sis scrutinized my behavior, watching for anything that might indicate we were going for a walk or ride. She knew that when I put on my tennis shoes, we were going for a walk and would immediately go into a frenzy. When I picked up my car keys or the leash Sis would make a dash to the door. She led me by the leash many times on our walks. Sis did not care if we walked on cement or dirt; she made our walks an adventure.

Sis meandered, like a child, looking over anything and everything in her path. She would linger; a bush had to be smelled, a tree had to be circled for scents, a fire hydrant had to be watered. Like all dogs, Sis had to leave her "mark" on the world; urinating to leave her scent for other dogs or covering the scent of another dog.

In those seventeen years of her existence, I learned to walk fast and to walk long distances. I learned to walk daily.

I learned to take in my surroundings and enjoy the beauty of nature. I also lowered my blood pressure and stress. The regular exercise helped, but research has shown even petting an animal has a calming effect.

I still walk long distances, a habit I continue from my time with Sis. She taught me how to be healthy; to take time and smell the roses (so to say). I learned more from Sis than from any health guru or book.

A Compassionate Presence

Compassion means to "suffer with." When we are with others in their pain, we empathize with them. We walk the journey of letting go of our loved ones with a loving heart. Compassion was a lesson I learned from Sis.

Aging is a fact of life and dogs are no exception to this fact. Sis was aging sooner than I wanted. Accustomed to walking two to three miles a day, in the last few years of her life, she could only manage a mile or less.

Arthritis set in and she was no longer able to jump up on the bed. The exterior steps were hard for her to climb. Eventually, getting up from the floor to a sitting position required more effort.

After all those years of relying on Sis for her companionship, energy and zest, I was able to return the favor. Sis came to rely on me to carry her up and down the steps. I would push her buttocks to help her stand up and dispensed baby aspirins and arthritis pills to ease the pain.

Sis struggled with other problems associated with aging. Poodles are prone to getting bumps or lesions on their skin and Sis developed a huge growth on her nose during the last seven years of her life. This had to be watched to ensure it did not grow too large or become malignant.

Sis' eyesight also began to fail as she developed cataracts and became farsighted. Her hearing was also fading so I used hand signals and clapped to get her attention. One sense, however, remains longer with dogs as they age. Sis' eyesight was failing and her hearing and mobility became impaired but she maintained her sense of smell.

In the last two years of her life Sis developed pancreatitis, an inflammatory abdominal ailment. Think of the worse stomachache you ever experienced—that is what it feels like. Treatment included overnight stays at the veterinarian for intravenous feeding along with a complete change in diet. Dog treats and human food were off limits. Small portions of hamburger and rice were fed to her several times a day with ice for water.

There were days when she could not eat. I would rock her in the chair on a blanket, feeling her pain. Sis also developed a cognitive disorder. In human terms it can be likened to Alzheimer's disease. Her behavior became unpredictable.

Disoriented, she would wander into the street or she would stand in the corner of a room for a long time. I would have to wake her up as she slept long hours. She still knew who I was and would come to me, putting her head on my lap, but she no longer greeted me at the door.

Early one morning I was awakend by a noise. I jumped out of bed looking for Sis. I found her in a corner. She was groaning so I picked her up to hold her. She upchucked all over me. When I tried to set her down, she could not move on her legs. I held her for a long time.

I took her to the vet who examined her. Believing Sis had suffered a stroke, the vet injected her with medicine. For twenty-four hours after that, Sis did not eat or drink or even move from her blanket. A day later she got up and appeared to have recovered from her stroke.

The vet cautioned that dogs, like humans, can have multiple strokes. The blood vessels in the brain are smaller so they can clog faster. I would need to watch Sis for further signs of stroke.

Several weeks later when Sis was outdoors she fell over the curb. Running to pick her up I noticed her eyes were closed; a mucus had formed. A side effect of the stroke, her tear ducts had dried up. She would require drops and ointments twice daily to help her dry eyes. She also lost her peripheral vision in her right eye, as a result of the stroke. Her right eye drooped like Bell's Palsy.

A final indignity of aging was the loss of bladder control. Sis could no longer control herself. Months before she had been able to hold her bladder for up to twelve hours. No more. She would go outdoors but still relieve herself inside. Her inability to remember to properly discharge outdoors was no doubt due to her cognitive impairment. Sis slept more so I bought "pee" pads, which she often slept on.

Sis continued to experience setbacks from the pancreatitis and would have times when she would not eat for several days. Her diet was changed to a "senior" dog food, specifically designed for intestinal problems. She no longer ate during regular hours but would get hungry around midnight. She would eat but would fall asleep over her food. Eventually Sis could not eat standing up and had to lay down or be fed by me.

My mother died four and a half years later of a massive stroke; she shared a similar experience as Sis. A massive stroke with small strokes over the last four years reduced her to a life of helplessness from a loss of bladder and bowel control as well as a loss of sensory stimulation.

It is difficult to see a loved one age and suffer. We feel helpless knowing we can do no more. Life is filled with losses which we endure until we experience that deeper loss, from which there is no recovery—death.

Surrendering

It is better to have loved and lost,
than not to have loved at all.
—William Shakespeare

A wise nun once said to me, "God forgive us if we ever forget each other." August 9, 2000, is a day I will never forget; it was the day Sis died. I spent the day sitting with her on the floor, petting her while she slept. I prayed to commend Sis into God's hands.

At 2:30 p.m. several friends and family accompanied me to take Sis to the vet to be euthanized. Sis' health condition at age seventeen was deteriorating. I sprinkled Sis with holy water and anointed her with perfumed oils made from the Poor Clare Monastery.

I held Sis in my arms while we sang the refrain from "On Eagle's Wings" based on Psalm 91 by Michael Joncas.

And he will raise you up on eagle's wings
Bear you on the breath of dawn
Make you to shine like the sun
And hold you in the palm of his hand.

For to his angels he's given a command
To guard you in all of your ways
Upon their hands they will bear you up
Lest you dash your foot against a stone.

Sis died in my arms. The assistant placed Sis in her "coffin," a plastic container with her blanket, her favorite stuffed dog she had since she was a pup, her leash and collar and the pullover sweater she wore for her winter walks.

We buried Sis under a hickory tree by a flowering bush, overlooking a prairie. The burial ritual was woven with memories of Sis. The grave is marked with a rock etched with the words, "Sis Blum, December 16, 1983 – August 9, 2000."

Death is a separation from loved ones. Death is a letting go. Death is surrendering. It is not easy; mourning remains with us to the end of our days.

The last part of the poem by Mary Oliver, *In Blackwater Woods*, sums up my feelings at the time.

Every year
Everything I have ever learned
In my lifetime
Leads back to this:
The fires and the black river of loss
Whose other side is salvation
Whose meaning
None of us will ever know.

To live in this world
You must be able
To do three things:
To love what is mortal
To hold it
Against your bones
Knowing your own life depends on it
And when the time comes
To let it go
To let it go.

Life goes on. Time heals. Reality sets in. Get up to go to work. Activities fill the days. Hedged in the day and the night times are memories. Memories keep alive the loved one with whom we shared life. To "re-member" connects us with the presence of the other. Someone shared this wisdom with me, "Grief is as deep as the person you love."

We have pictures and we have stories. It is important to share those stories, to tell them and retell them. We learn from the stories about life. We learn that living is relational. We learn that we need relationships to find meaning in life.

When we find a friend we find meaning in life. When we find meaning in life, we find God. Relationships begin at birth but do not end with death—for a friend lives within us. Sis left her paw prints in my heart. Death does not completely separate us from our loved ones. Instead, a new kind of life begins.

A Dog Is A Faithful Friend

A faithful friend is a sure shelter,
whoever finds one has found a rare treasure.
—Ecclesiasticus 6:5

Written and oral stories abound where dogs exhibit faithfulness to an owner. A dog can be seen guarding a family member. I recall a time when I was returning home outside the city limits and glimpsed a dog standing by the road. I tried to coax the dog into my car so I could find the owner. The dog would not budge.

The dog remained there. A few days later I came upon his dead body, still beside the road. An owner may drop off a dog in the country but the dog stays in the same place waiting for the owner to return. Faithful until death do us part.

I remember the Japanese story of Hitachi that was made into a movie. Hitachi was a dog who faithfully walked with his owner to and from the train station as the owner went to work. One day the owner had a fatal heart attack and did not return home. The faithful dog continued to walk to the train station to await the owner's return until, he too, died.

A dog is faithful to the end. Fidelity is at the heart of friendship. Sis was truly a friend. What more can one want?

Every year Sis was remembered in ritual on October 4, the Feast of St. Francis of Assisi who had a deep relationship with creation. *A Blessing Prayer for Pets* by Edward Hays was often read. I have adapted it by inserting Sis' name.

May we now bless Sis
By taking delight in her beauty and naturalness.
May we bless this animal
With a Noah-like protection
For all that might harm her.
May we, like Adam and Eve,
Speak to this creature of Yours
With kindness and affection,
Reverencing her life and purpose
In our communal creation.

May we never treat Sis as a dumb animal
But rather let us seek to learn her language
And to be a student of all the secrets that she knows.
May the Blessing of God rest upon this creature
Who will be a companion for us in the journey of life.

A Pet Companion

Stories come from memories of what we have lived. These stories can help us learn and can teach us lessons. I have learned many lessons about living from my journey with Sis, many I shared with you.

Sharing memories is a part of the healing process. I now invite you, dear reader, to reflect on your own memories of a beloved pet. What lessons have you learned from your own pets? Tell and retell the stories with a grateful heart.

> *Nothing can make up for the absence of someone whom we love...It is nonsense to say that God fills the gap. God doesn't fill it but on the contrary. God keeps it empty and so helps us to keep alive our former communion with each other even at the cost of pain...The dearer and richer the memories, the more difficult the separation.*
>
> *But gratitude changes the pangs of memory into tranquil joy. The beauties of the past are borne, not as a thorn in the flesh, but as a precious gift in themselves.*
> —Diedrich Bonhoeffer

My cherished memory is…

What I learned from my pet companion….

Sr. Marci with Sis (5 years old).

Sis with a snack (4 years old).

Sis as a pup chewing her rawhide.

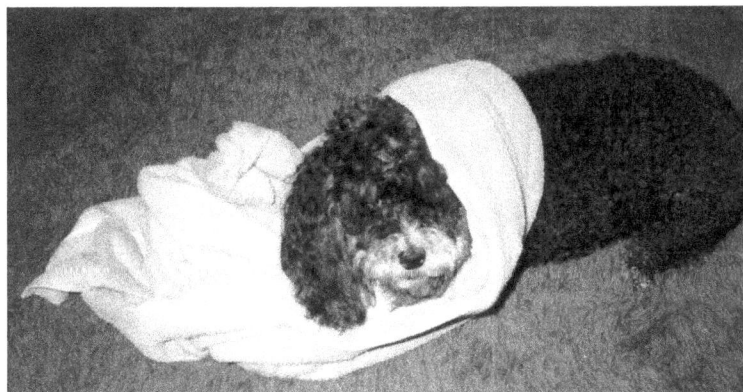

Sis playing with a towel (6 years old).

She's Not Heavy. She's my Sis.

Sis as a pup with her favorite stuffed animal
that was buried with her.

Sis relaxing after a trip to the dog groomer.

Sis posing for a photo (5 years old).

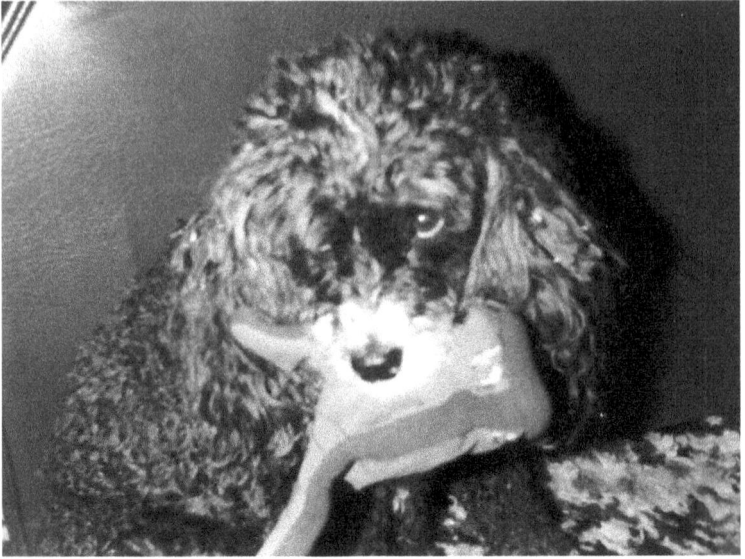

Sis playing with my glove.

Sis enjoying the flowers (4 years old).

Sis posing for her picture (3 years old).

After Sis died, friends inquired if I intended to adopt another dog. How could Sis be replaced? Thirteen months later, a dog breeder approached me about adopting one of her dogs who was not able to breed. I went to her place and could not resist a beautiful petite dog who spoke with her bright and gentle eyes.

Here is her story.

It's Okay, Rhea
A Story about Rhea

Nothing is so strong as gentleness;
Nothing so gentle as real strength.
  —St. Francis de Sales (16th century)

Three days before September 11, 2001, Rhea was in my arms. On the fateful day itself, I awoke with the radio blaring the sad news of the New York tragedy while Rhea's fearful eyes searched mine. It was as if she was asking "What am I doing here?" Two events collided in fear. One was the fear of the loss of the American lives. The other was Rhea's fear of loss of security in an unfamiliar home. I murmured to her, "It's okay, Rhea."

Two weeks prior, a dog breeder asked me if I was interested in having a four-year-old black toy poodle. The poodle had conceived three healthy male pups by caesarean but later had a rupture. Since she could no longer breed, the owner was willing to give the dog to me. I considered hard and long. The owner introduced me to the dog, then gave me the American Kennel papers with her official name, "Rhea of Stony Brook." I'll never forget the parting words by the dog breeder. "Rhea needs a gentle person and you two are a perfect fit." No truer words were spoken about Rhea. When I carried the poodle away the six-pounder looked back at her home of four years with fear in her eyes.

Why was the name Rhea given to her? I asked my cousin, Donna Bauerly, an English professor, who replied "Rhea was the name of the goddess mother of Zeus." Mother. That was Rhea who birthed three pups. That was Rhea who was so gentle and sweet. My little Rhea.

That first evening, while in the shower I heard the howl of a wolf. Rhea was standing in the middle of the dining room, her head raised skyward emitting a long lonely cry. For several days Rhea did not eat, no doubt a sign of her loneliness and insecurity.

Finally a friend brought her toy poodle, Raven, over to play with Rhea. Raven was a half-sister to Rhea. A piece of chicken was laid on the sofa to entice Rhea to eat. When Raven reached out for the chicken, Rhea growled to protect "her" piece of chicken from Raven. Later Rhea did eat.

When I discovered Rhea was not entirely housebroken at the age of four, I confined her to the kitchen with a gate when I left for work. Upon returning home, I found Rhea sleeping on the sofa. The "pee-pad" that was on the kitchen floor was crumpled and torn. Rhea had jumped the gate.

Needing to housebreak her, I tried to reward Rhea with a dog treat whenever she did her duty outdoors, but to no avail. Rhea evidently was not accustomed to dog treats, as she rarely ate dog treats throughout her time with me.

Eventually Rhea trained me. I learned that when Rhea would sniff the floor or walk around the room that it was time for me to let her outside to do her business.

The first four years of Rhea's life, she had been confined to a kennel. She was not accustomed to walking on the streets with cars speeding by. When I first began walking Rhea, she hesitated and would stop in her tracks when a car cruised by. The sight and sound of the cars frightened her.

We would go one step, pause, two steps, pause, three steps. "It's okay, Rhea." I would repeat. Each day we ventured forth further and further, finally, we went a block.

Rhea disliked the leash, so she followed me or stayed by my side as we walked. The amazing part of our initial walks was that Rhea did not seek out trees, fire hydrants or bushes to do her duty. She just walked. I encouraged her, "Rhea, you gotta 'go' when we walk. That's one of our purposes in walking." She just looked at me and kept on walking. After several daily walks she got the idea. She learned to stop and smell the fire hydrants along the sidewalk and leave her mark.

I took Rhea to the veterinarian for a check up soon after she became a member of our household. I was shocked when the veterinarian had to extract sixteen teeth that were decayed or loose. I learned later that small dogs are susceptible to losing teeth. I had tried to coax Rhea to chew on the "greenies" and other chewy dog treats that were supposed to keep her teeth strong, but again, Rhea wanted nothing to do with them. I even resorted to buying a beef bone. I boiled it and laid it in her dog dish. She licked it and walked away.

Over the years, Rhea had more teeth removed. Eventually her six remaining teeth had to be pulled. The vet reassured me that removal of her teeth would not affect her eating habits. Rhea always had a long tongue, noticeably visible in a little body. With her teeth removed, her tongue generally hung outside her mouth. Where else would a tongue rest other than on a lower set of teeth in the mouth?

Gradually her lip sagged to the right and grew more sensitive to touch by the dog groomer. As Rhea aged, I found that she did not eat as much. Rhea, I noted, had a hard time keeping food in her mouth without teeth.

I was troubled by a behavior pattern with Rhea when I first brought her home. I would reach down to pet her but Rhea reflexively yelped and moved away. She acted like she thought I was going to hit her.

In Rhea's previous home there lived several cats and a number of dogs who barked often and loud. When I first visited her previous home, I saw dogs confined to kennels in the kitchen, the dining room, and dogs in kennels outside.

Several litters of poodles, pugs and other breeds were kept in these kennels.

The dog breeder would swat the dogs with her hand to get them to stop barking, and the dog would cower. I was surprised by this but realized this was the cause of Rhea's behavior. After about six months, Rhea finally realized I was not going to hurt her and she no longer cringed when I petted her. "The hand that pets is not to be the hand that hits."

Rhea was, in general, a very timid dog and trembled when she met people. Was this because she was kenneled and did not meet a diversity of people in her previous place? She may have been shy by personality; yet the environment may have added to her shyness.

I deliberately took Rhea for rides, which she loved, and introduced her to new people so she could become more socialized. I reassured her on these visits, "It's okay, Rhea." As the years went by Rhea would approach people on her own.

Rhea's fears were most apparent when she heard loud, unexpected noises. She would tremble and shake during thunderstorms. My sleep was interrupted many nights because of her fear of thunder. I would awaken to Rhea pacing on the bed and shaking. Although window blinds were closed, she still saw the bright flashes of lightning. My ritual of turning on both the radio and the lights helped.

Some nights I held her and walked through the house, keeping away from the windows. Other nights Rhea would crawl under the covers trying to escape the sound. I would reassure her. "It's okay, Rhea," and hoped it helped.

She maintained these fears throughout her life. I called Rhea my "doppler radar" because she sensed a storm before it even arrived. I did some research and discovered that some dogs have the ability to forecast a storm. Elizabeth Bishop wrote a poem that makes me think of Rhea: "Think of the storm roaming the sky uneasily like a dog looking for a place to sleep in, listen to it growling."

Fireworks were another source of distress for Rhea. I began to dread the the Fourth of July . The neighbors lit Roman candles, firecrackers or whatever and Rhea would shiver and shake. It became a routine to head to Minneapolis, where my family lived in a quiet cul-de-sac neighborhood. Their well-insulated home kept out the noise of celebration and Rhea was able to relax.

Loud or sudden noises of any kind disrupted Rhea's equilibrium. When anyone, including me, would sneeze or cough, she was out of the room lickety-split. To this day, whenever I cough or sneeze I think of Rhea.

Over the years, eating continued to be difficult for Rhea. Sometimes I had to hand feed her to make sure she ate. At times she shunned eating for a day or more even though her stomach would be growling.

I consulted my veterinarian and she suggested feeding her IAMS intestinal dog food—dry or canned dog food—that is bought only from a veterinarian. Rhea did eat that type of food, but not always. The most Rhea ever weighed was 7-7 ½ pounds.

Rhea loved to ride in the car. Whenever she saw me pick up the car keys, she ran to the door, ready to travel. She would sit on my lap while I drove. People asked if she ever moved off my lap, but she never did, even on the five hour trips to Minneapolis. Luckily, no accidents occurred with Rhea on my driver's lap.

Visiting family during Thanksgiving in Minneapolis was always fun. One year we had four dogs in the house—Rhea, my sister's miniature poodles, Ginny and Johnny, and my nephew-in-law's Boston Terrier, Bruno.

Bruno was an active dog running around the house. Rhea, who was much smaller than Bruno, tore after Bruno, then cornered and growled at him. Bruno immediately settled down. She surprised many, including me! "That is okay, Rhea!"

I expected a barking dog since Rhea was a poodle, but she only barked when someone came to the door or at people or animals that were near the house. She barked only as a warning; she never bared her teeth (when she had them). Rhea did not have a mean bone in her body.

I see Rhea running down the sidewalk, her ears flying in the air. So alive. "It's okay to be free, Rhea." In our back yard Rhea spied a squirrel. She crept closer and began the chase. Midway through the speedy run, she braked, turned around and looked to me for affirmation. "It's okay, Rhea."

Often on our walks she would amble up the steps to people's houses, look around to me for acquiescence. "Not okay, Rhea." Rhea became so free that she would walk off by herself to explore. She never ran away but finally felt confident to explore by herself without prodding from me. "That's okay, Rhea."

Rhea spent nine years of her life with Katy, my roommate's cat. When Katy joined the household, true to a cat's curious nature, she walked all through the house. Rhea followed her as she roamed the closets and corners of the rooms. After some intial negative encounters, they were able to get along.

One day timid Rhea wanted to walk through the threshold to the kitchen but Katy was lying by the doorway. Rhea hesitated when she saw Katy, but decided to venture forth. Sure enough, when she walked past Katy, she swatted Rhea on her behind. Katy would also chase Rhea, at least until the time Rhea stopped running, turned to Katy and stared. That was the last time Katy chased Rhea. Eventually they became friends and would sleep next to each other on the floor in the afternoon sun.

Rhea lived with me over ten years, seldom needing to see the vetrinarian other than for immunizations. That changed in July 2011. Rhea began to have problems with eating, loose bowels and vomiting.

The veterinarian examined Rhea and found a heart murmur in addition to the stomach problem. The veterinarian gave medicine and Rhea eventually regained some of her appetite. She now weighed only four and one-half pounds, a loss of one and one-half pounds.

When Rhea became wobbly on her feet while walking, I contacted a veterinarian friend of mine. He offered to examine Rhea in September free of charge. An x-ray, blood test and an EKG revealed that Rhea had an enlarged heart. A big heart for little Rhea.

My vet friend provided heart medication for Rhea. Since she does not swallow pills well, medication was provided in liquid form. The vet asked, "What flavor do you want? Beef, chicken or salmon?" I responded for Rhea, "Chicken." In the morning and in the evening, I inserted three syringes in Rhea's mouth to help regulate her blood pressure, heart beat and fluid retention. The x-ray also showed that her kidneys were not operating well. By September, Rhea weighed only four pounds.

In December, Rhea had another set back. She did not eat for several days and whatever food she did eat did not stay down. The vet took blood tests and found her kidneys were not functioning and she was dehydrated. For two days she received fluids. The vet gave me Nutrical, a gel tube with vitamins, to provide energy. It worked. I gave her a one-half teaspoon, twice a day. Her eating seemed to improve and her appetite was better. I stayed home for Christmas to be with her.

By the end of February, Rhea again was not feeling well. She did not eat for five days. Eventually she was able to keep some food down. On February 28, 2012, Rhea went back to the vet. She was dehydrated again, her heart was not beating well, and her weight was down to 2.4 pounds.

With tears streaming down my cheeks, the vet and I discussed her health condition. Would she get better? Do I want her to suffer? For six months Rhea's heart medication helped her but now her kidneys were not able to function.

The vet took us into a private room where she injected anesthesia in Rhea, the kind before surgery. I held Rhea on my lap until she fell asleep. The vet returned to the room and she shaved Rhea's front leg in preparation for euthanasia. It only took minutes and Rhea was dead on my lap.

Tears, tears, and more tears flowed. I held Rhea for a long time. The vet brought out a box with a blanket inside to lay Rhea in. On April 1, 2012, Rhea would have been 15 years old.

Of the many sympathy notes and condolences sent to me, one story in particular touched me deeply. A veterinarian was called to a home of a family whose older dog was dying of cancer. The couple thought that their six-year-old boy might learn something by being present for the euthanasia procedure. The little boy seemed so calm, petting the old dog for the last time. Within a few minutes, the dog slipped peacefully away. The little boy seemed to accept the dying process of his dog.

After the dog's death, the family sat around the table with the veterinarian wondering about the sad fact that animal lives are shorter than human lives. The little boy, who had been listening quietly, piped up, ''I know why. People are born so that they can learn how to live a good life—like loving everybody all the time and being nice, right?'' The six-year-old continued, "Well, dogs already know how to do that, so they don't have to stay as long."

Rhea was buried on the grounds of Shalom Retreat Center. A group of friends gathered to share memories of Rhea and to pray with the words of Fr. Ed Hayes from his book, *Prayers for the Domestic Church*. I have adapted it by inserting Rhea's name.

It's Ok, Rhea
Prayer at the Death of a Family Pet

Lord God,
to those who have never had a pet, this prayer will sound
strange, but to you, Lord of All Life and Creator of All
Creatures, it will be understandable.

Our hearts are heavy as we face the loss in death of our
beloved Rhea who was so much a part of our lives.

Rhea made our lives more enjoyable and gave us cause to
thank You and to find joy in her company.

We remember the faithfulness and trust of Rhea and will miss
her presence in our home.

From her we learned many lessons such as gentleness and
strength and her request for affection.

In caring for her daily needs, we were taken up out of our own
self-needs and thus learned to serve another.

May the loss of Rhea remind us that death comes to all of us,
animal and human, and that it is the natural passage for all life.

May Rhea sleep on in an eternal slumber in Your Godly Care
as all creation awaits the Fullness of Life.

Amen.

Rhea lived with me for over ten years. She was a special dog. She was a gentle dog who sensed what to do and be. I never had to correct her behavior. She was gentle, but she was strong. That seems to be a paradox. To me it is a sign of maturity—to hold opposites together. I learned from Rhea that gentleness is strength and strength is gentleness. That is a wisdom that will remain with me.

I can hear Rhea saying, "It's okay, Marci." Thank you, Rhea, for sharing your life and love with me

Rhea